BRAZIL

TRAVEL GUIDE FOR MEN

TRAVEL BRAZIL LIKE YOU REALLY WANT TO!

Christopher Street

TABLE OF CONTENTS

INTRODUCTION

The very word 'Brazil' is a sexy one – it's fixating on big hips at the carnival, hot bodies in the sun at the Copacabana, and women known the world over for their beauty and openness.

It's the 'Brazilian' – revealing underwear and everything smooth to perfection from the waist down.

There's a reason for this and it's because Brazil offers men experiences like nowhere else in the world and in this guide we're going to show you how to get the most out of this country.

Brazil is a country of dazzling variety from its jungles to its beaches to its mountains. It has some of the most vibrant cities in the world and is beloved by many for its relaxing culture and warmness.

In this guide we hope to show you how this is true for all parts of Brazil including its sex scene so we can lead you in finding the best clubs and making sure you have a good time.

Using this guide

Whether you want to meet escorts in a motel, find girls at a club, scout the streets, or just have a quick visit to a parlor we've got you covered. From the shining beacon that is Rio de Janeiro, through to Sao Paulo, Fortaleza, and the best beach cities Brazil has to offer.

We'll tell you the best ways to get in and out, where to stay and how to get around, how to stay safe and have fun, and the best spots to find girls.

Brazil is a cheap place when it wants to be but this doesn't mean you have to stay in flea bitten hostels and wash yourself down in a sink each night.

Enjoy luxury with some of the sexiest girls in the world while keeping it all in budget with our Brazil travel guide for men.

So *bem vinda* to Brazil and enjoy your stay.

WHY MEN LOVE BRAZIL

'Sex tourism' is an ugly phrase that tries to shame men and conjures up images of sad loners flying halfway around the world to pay girls to have sex with them because they can't get any at home.

It's an idea that comes from a wider culture of shame about sex (especially male sexuality) and a refusal to acknowledge that sex could be a real service you could offer people, or that there may be genuine reasons for men to seek out 'sex tourism'.

How the rest of the world does sex

In some parts of the world though, 'sex tourism' is a fitting word. You go to the streets of Amsterdam, you pick out girls from behind their windows, and then you haggle with a sour-faced prostitute about money before she leads you into a sterile sex booth where you aren't allowed to touch her body.

She may as well put on rubber gloves and handle your junk with a pair of salad tongs for all the romance there is involved. A 15-minute egg timer is put on before the fun begins and at the first sign of cum you are shooed out into the street and your trousers thrown out after you.

Here you are just buying sex and there's little difference between it and getting a haircut or going to the dentist. This is intentional in places like Europe and Australia where legalization was done to try and kill the industry.

If you want anything more than that you have to explicitly seek out 'the girlfriend experience' and a lot of the time that is just code for kissing on the lips and a blowjob without a condom.

Despite it being legal in these places it's still not socially acceptable.

It's a little better in parts of South East Asia like Thailand because working girls do see fostering a relationship with a man as part of the service they offer.

You are paying more for her time which includes sex rather than just paying her to perform a sex act. You aren't treated as just a punter, but a potential lover.

Yet Thailand has many of its own problems when it comes to its sex industry and is rife with scammers making it hard to navigate things if you are there on holiday.

How Brazil does sex

In Brazil the line between romance and sex worker is blurred. If you want you can opt for a quick bang or blowjob in a back alley bedroom but doing so is no big deal for anyone.

The fact you can do that so cheaply, without shame, and with relative ease changes things for the scene in Brazil. When you go to meet other working girls they will approach you like someone they want to be with and with a completely different attitudes about what paying for sex means.

In Brazil you will find these girls are offering to be your companion and to spend time with you and not just with a complete fixation at what's in your wallet.

At no point in meeting a sex worker in Europe will you ever believe the girl is attracted to you, or even likes you. In Brazil you won't be sure if she even wants you to pay her.

This is why men from all over the world pay to come to Brazil when they can easily pay for sex legally at home. For a while they can feel like sex gods or celebrities where for the first time in their lives attractive women are approaching them and not just to game them, but to spend time with them.

When it does come to having sex you can take someone who makes you feel good back to a comfortable place and make love at your leisure and in a way that feels more respectful to the both of you.

Having a girl stay with you for the night is the norm and you end things with a kiss rather than a shakedown.

Get ready for the time of your life because when you come here you may not want to leave.

PLANNING YOUR TRIP

Brazil is a fascinating and beautiful country that you should try to explore as much you can from its fascinating beaches to its dense jungles.

When you're planning a man's trip though, a real sexy one, the question of planning becomes quite different to just seeing the big sites. Going from town to town and city to city to find different girls and clubs is exciting but you do have to be realistic, there are literally millions of sex workers in Brazil and they are located all over.

You can only have sex with so many of them and wherever you go it is ultimately you who will have sex with the women and create the experience.

Trying to hunt down magical girls might leave you feeling a bit like Ahab looking for his white whale. You'll get told all sorts of things about how Fortaleza or Natal or Rio has the best girls and not to waste your time with Sao Paulo or Florianopolis because you'll just get ripped off.

However, there is no perfect location and you should plan your itinerary around the things you want to do and see and where is cheapest to get to. In this guide we're going to look at the scenes in some of Brazil's biggest coastal cities and some of its best sex scenes including Rio de Janeiro, Recife, Fortaleza, Salvador, and Sao Paulo.

Brazil lives for its coastline and although some of its most important cities like its capital Brasilia are more inland, it is in these places that you will find the best talent on display and the most competition out looking to please you.

Many of these places exist in their own right as beach resorts and are worth visiting if you just want to chill out, but since this is where tourists and travelers come it's also where the girls come. Here you will find the best clubs, sex beaches, and largest variety of escorts available.

The biggest and most popular cities Rio and Sao Paulo have the most choice in terms of girls and services, but they are also increasingly becoming the most expensive. The ability to pick up a temporary girlfriend for your stay is becoming less and less common as girls start to treat sex as more of a Western commodity.

If you want the more traditional 'no-watching-the-clock' feel then you will want to take a dip into a smaller resort like Recife or Fortaleza. Go too far away from the tourist rough though and you'll find there aren't as many girls on offer and less of a scene in general.

If you're just coming here for the girls it might be best to set aside a lot of money for Rio (which has a scene all of its own) and general sightseeing before choosing a smaller town to wind down in for a week or two. Get the best of both worlds and discover what Brazil really has to offer.

GETTING TO BRAZIL

Unless you live in South America getting to Brazil is not usually cheap or easy for anyone. This is why getting the most out of your time there is so important because it's not like a quick dip into Tijuana.

If you are flying from the USA then flights from Florida and New York tend to be cheapest with some one way tickets from Miami going for as little as $300. Sao Paulo and Rio predictably have the biggest airports, but often cheapest the destinations are smaller airports like Manaus and Belem.

The reason for this is that they are located in the poorer north of Brazil and aren't really popular travel destinations and nor are they on the coast.

Manaus is a good launching platform for getting into the Amazon rainforest, but Brazil is an enormous country and it is unlikely to cut your costs down for moving on to Rio or other large cities (though it won't make it more expensive if you want to split the trip up).

Manaus is, however, cheaper than many other regions and has its own fun in the jungle scene.

Belem is closer to the coast and you can get relatively cheap flights to Fortaleza, Natal, or Recife. Nevertheless, it would still take a day's bus ride to get to any of these locations. Belem is a touch cheaper than some of these other cities and has many of the same features, but it is still an inconvenience to be out of the way here.

If you happen to live in Florida and you only care about being in Brazil then going to Belem for a week might be worth it. But Belem does not really compete with the other cities in this guide.

For most people coming from the USA flying into Rio first is the most cost effective option and from there flying on to another of the main cities. In Brazil taking a long distance bus can be a bit of a false economy as spending a day or two moving between cities is a day or two of partying you lose out on. There is not much of a rail network to rely on either.

From Europe it is a slightly different picture. Flying into Salvador, Natal or Recife might actually work out cheaper than flying immediately to Rio. If you do want to fly direct you will most likely need to travel from Portugal or Germany and again you will be limited to Salvador, Recife, and Fortaleza for direct flights.

Prices one way from Europe start at around €250 from Portugal in the less busy seasons.

THE BEST TIME TO VISIT BRAZIL

The first thing to keep in mind is that Brazil is in the southern hemisphere so it's got its weather and seasons on backwards. Yet this switch needn't concern you greatly as it is generally warm throughout the year.

The climate around the country varies with it being warmer in the north and cooler in the south especially in Sao Paulo which actually gets mild winters. In a lot of the northern coastal cities the weather will rarely be lower than the mid twenties in Celsius. Though if you come in the northern hemisphere's 'winter' (December to March) things will be hotter than the rest of the year.

Once you leave the coast there is a more distinct dry and wet season – especially in the rainforest areas. October to January is seen as the wet season for the Rio area even if it doesn't rain very frequently, and from April to July in the northern coastal cities like Fortaleza, Recife, and Salvador.

It may not rain frequently as it might in more temperate climates but it can rain very intensely and even cause flooding in some regions.

Planning around the weather shouldn't be a huge concern if you avoid the heights of summer and the rainy season (though you shouldn't fear them too much).

The sweet spot for many people will be between April and November in terms of bodies and weather. Brazilians typically get December and January off for holidays and school holidays, and New Year's Eve and Carnival in February-March are enormous celebrations that make the country very busy all over.

In terms of working girls off-seasons can be a very good time to visit. You'll have a better pick, less competitive rates, and fewer tourists to move around.

THE SKINNY ON PROSTITUTION IN BRAZIL

Paying for sex in Brazil is perfectly legal and you don't have to worry about breaking any laws so long as you use common sense and don't do anything that is clearly dodgy. If a girl doesn't seem like she is comfortable or happy then don't pursue her – if she seems drugged up or under age then run very far away.

Brothels are technically illegal in Brazil and if you have sex with a girl at a club or parlor you will be going with a girl that in theory works for herself. However, brothels or private houses where you can have sex with girls that are operated by more-or-less pimps are very common. The idea there is that the girls are just renting space in the brothel and they are still independent. Many girls are freelancers or independent but many have 'management' as well.

Working girls and guys aren't regulated in any way by the government so it's not necessarily safe to assume STDs are being kept under control as they might be in a place like the Netherlands. You might be expected to pay to use condoms in some clubs and by most girls which will be on offer, but always carry some of your own just in case.

Prostitution is however a recognized profession in Brazil and fairly common, so don't feel pressured into paying more for something shady if you know it's legal to do it. As a gringo you will be targeted by girls for more money and you should expect to pay a little extra, but you shouldn't be ripped off or threatened.

THE SCENE

Brazil does thing a little differently to the rest of the world when it comes to its sex scene. You can find girls on the street if you wish to, but there is not a huge advantage to this and things work a little more like they do in Thailand.

The most common method of operation is to choose a club, bathhouse, or bar where the freelance working girls reside. You generally pay an entrance fee and you are expected to want to enjoy the facilities in the places you go to including using the bars, visiting the saunas, or eating the food.

You then speak to and flirt with a girl before taking her away to a room provided or going to a 'love motel' where you pay for a room by the hour. Initial prices can seem cheaper because there are a lot of rental costs involved which you pay for such as the room, towels, or condoms (which thankfully aren't rented).

Many hotels will not let you take girls back with you and if you intend to do that then make sure to ask if you are allowed 'guests' in your room first. They may not do anything if you try to bring a girl back anyway, but if they notice it might be embarrassing for you.

Asking to spend the night with a girl is fairly common and extras such as anal or CIM (cum in mouth) are commonplace as well, even if you have to pay extra. You may even spend extra time with a girl and arrange to see her again without it necessarily being paid for (although if you have sex with her again – do expect to pay for it).

Different cities have different reputations and procedures when it comes to the girls. Some say that in Rio the girls are more open but will charge you more and are more likely to rip you off. In Sao Paulo they are more likely to have better services and facilities, but things like anal will always costs you extra and are not a given.

As Rio is by far the most popular destination when we are discussing the scene in this first part of the guide we will be talking about what goes on in Rio, but what is true here is broadly true for the rest of Brazil.

As a rule of thumb the more south you in Brazil the whiter the people become as the white Europeans settled more in the south of the country (think German-looking). If you are interested in darker skinned girls you will need to go the north of the country. Rio is a mixed bag and you will be able to find girls from across the globe here if that is what you are after.

There is a caveat here though which is that the girls nearly all speak Portuguese and if she's speaking English it means she knows what she's worth. It's best to brush up on a few phrases before you go and maybe keep a translator handy.

THE SEVEN TYPES OF GIRLS YOU WILL MEET IN BRAZIL

There are several different approaches to finding girls to play with in Brazil and here we're going to run down some of the most common to look out for and try your hand at. Even if you are not entirely sure what is happening if gesture to your crotch enough you'll probably end up in bed with a girl at some point.

BOITES (SEX NIGHTCLUBS)

These sex clubs are what set Brazil a little apart from the rest of the world as you won't find their similarity in a lot of places. You pay an entry fee (it usually gets more expensive later on) and on the inside it looks like a regular club you'd find in the rest of the city or even back home.

Dancing girls, crappy pop music blaring out of the speakers, awkward guys in the corner, and a well stocked bar. The difference here is that every girl is available to be whisked away to a motel or room after a little bit of negotiation.

If you like the look of a girl you don't just point her out and shepherd into a backroom for some hanky-panky. You catch her attention, buy her a drink if you like (though be careful as you can get stung with the prices), and maybe even do some dirty dancing. Feel free to have a try with different girls you are interested in.

You may find that some of the girls even approach you if they are interested – rumor has it that cute guys with a lot of charm will get severely reduced rates. The girls at these bars do often do genuinely appear to be enjoying themselves and they will make you feel like they want to dance with you.

If you've been to a nightclub back home and been disappointed at what happened then the clubs here are basically your fantasies come true. It is a dance hall full of sexy women that won't turn you down and are all willing to go home with you.

Once you found a girl a like you'll have to start talking money. Gringos always pay more – especially if you look rich but throughout most of the country r100 is a doable price for an hour of fun. If you are looking to save money try to pick girls that look like they'd be happier with less.

When you are ready to go and have haggled away you usually need to pay a 'bar fine' on top of her fee. In many clubs you will then take a taxi to a motel or your hotel, or you might be able to use a room at the club.

When you are negotiating you can haggle on the price, ask for extras, and suggest she stay the night if you want.

The range of sex clubs varies enormously from city to city. The most famous in Rio for a long time was the club Help which would have as many as 400 girls to pick from there on any given night.

You may also find some smaller clubs with a few older girls hanging around the bar and some grimy rooms in the back you wouldn't enter without some hand sanitizer and a gasmask. Choose wisely.

STRIP CLUBS

The strip clubs in Brazil work like a mix between the typical clubs you'd find in Europe or the USA mixed with the sex clubs above. There may or may not be a cover fee and there will almost be overpriced drinks (by Brazilian standards) There are girls dancing at their poles and sometimes even putting on a live sex show.

If you are interested you can speak to one of the girls who will usually be happy to negotiate a price with you and then take an early night with you. These are usually a mixed bag and you can't always be certain the girls are all 'working' when you go inside, but finding out isn't any more difficult than speaking to one of the girls.

TERMAS (SEX SPAS)

Termas are one of the most coveted sex joints in Brazil because they offer a truly unique experience in comparison to many other scenes around the world. They are most similar to the FKK clubs you find in Germany, but are likely a little closer to the experience you dreamt of.

You pay a cover fee to enter and then you must put all your things in a locker and replace your clubbing clobber for a bath robe. Once you are inside you have a tab that mounts up as you get girls and drinks and you don't pay up until you're heading out the door.

Different termas have different facilities on offer. They are usually built like a regular spa with a bar and club attached. You can hang out in the hot tub or the sauna for a while if you like, or even get a regular massage to relax.

It might be a good time to wind down and get pampered by using some of the cleaning utensils that are on hand. Some of the termas are very fancy and built for the well-to-do business men of Brazil that want to use them. Don't rush for the girls; enjoy all the things you've paid for first.

But all of this is leading up the girls that are usually waiting in the bar and dancing around in only a few more garments than you currently have on. The girls are what people go crazy over with the termas and good girls can make one and bad girls will leave them empty.

In comparison to a lot of the other options and venues the girls here are often young, very good looking, and there to give you a good time not just a quick fuck and suck before setting you back out into the streets. Most terms try to have a good selection of girls to accommodate all tastes and if you want to be assured of a good lay with a hot chica then you won't do much better than a terma.

Once you have seen the talent eye up a girl you like and she will approach you for some flirting and foreplay. She might ask you to buy her a drink and will require a little bit of playful seduction to have a really good experience.

Wild groping or having too much fun in the bar is not really the thing to do, but touching, caressing and even kissing are all kosher. The girls only get paid from what you give them for sex in their rooms or cabines, so you can expect them to get very touchy-feely even under your robes.

The further along they get you, the more likely you are to say yes. Once you've agreed your price they will walk you to their room once it is empty and there you will usually have an hour. This includes showering and then whatever else it was you agreed on. When your time is up a phone will ring and if you got on especially well with the girl you might have a companion for the rest of your trip.

Besides the generally relaxed atmosphere and the good choice of girls what you really get here is security and assurance. Nothing sour is going to happen in regard to money or getting scammed and you often don't pay much more than you would elsewhere after you take into account a love hotel, taxi, and cover charge.

GIRLY BARS AND RESTAURANTS

Especially along the beachfronts in Rio and other resorts you will find bars and restaurants where you can lounge for the day and independent girls will wander in and you can eye them up and have a chat if you are interested in them.

It might be hard to hunt these down if you don't know where you are looking and some regular beach restaurants and bars may give you what you are after as well. When you've spoken to a girl you like and negotiated a price you can walk out of the place without any bar fine and take her somewhere nice.

There are also various bars around Brazil that operate in much the same way. In fact a lot of legitimate nightclubs and bars will have working girls in there among civilians out to enjoy the night.

You might be thinking, why would you ever go to a club if you can hang out on the beach and find girls cheaper? Well, that bar fine you'd usually is for a reason. The girls at these places are often not the most desirable girls in the city and you are not going to get the same kind of variety or choice here.

These places tend to be open more during the night and during the day you can find the girls elsewhere.

SEX BEACHES

You might hear these being called 'hooker beaches' or similar. There are working girls wandering up and down the beach quite a lot but certain parts of the beach have been organized more for working girls to meet clients.

When you turn up you'll find guys wanting to give you chairs, bring you girls, and get drinks from the bar for you. These guys are touts who are just looking to skim money off the whole thing and you can ignore them or just agree a price for something (like a chair) before you sit down.

You can get your own drinks from the bars and introduce to the girls that are standing around looking for guys. These are effectively just organized street girls so you don't need to worry too much about paying fines or anything else.

STREET AND BEACH GIRLS

It can be a little difficult to pick out working girls from regular girls when you are on the beach because a bikini is a bikini and Brazilians are in general not known for being prudish or too concerned with conservative attire at the beach.

Having said that, hookers in Brazil will generally look like you would imagine they do. If a scantily clad lady is stood around looking not too busy or preoccupied then it's likely she is down to clown.

Feel free to give her a nod or approach her in a friendly way and see where it leads you. There is no need to go too hard with the girls here as gringos in general are generally a magnet for attention.

Regular Brazilian girls are not idiots that can't take care of themselves so they are not going to reciprocate your actions if they are not working girls. The problem is that girls who aren't pushing themselves on you more aren't likely to speak much English.

Street girls tend to be working the street for a reason and when it comes to paying for sex in a poorer country hunting a bargain is rarely worth it. It's not always the case that a club or terma is a scam to squeeze more money out of you by putting in shiny lights and a middle man. In the clubs girls on drugs are generally a big no-no, on the streets anything can happen.

If you want success, safety, and ease of communication then street girls shouldn't be your primary focus. Nevertheless, don't be shy if you see a girl you like and she's happy to be given attention.

The huge range of girls in the rest of the city not enough for you? If you fancy ordering up a girl direct to your hotel or motel then there are lots of options.

As in many parts of the world you'll see classified adverts in newspapers and magazines, but you'll need to speak Portuguese to read them and they're on the way out in modern times.

The other option is to find a website with listing, galleries and contact details of girls online. Each city will have their own and the girls there may be the same ones you see in the clubs and on the street. The pictures aren't usually too accurate and the ages listed might be a few years out, however if you can get by in Portuguese or there is an email section where you can use Google translate it is quite good to use escort services.

Prices are largely the same online and you can discuss what you want more openly and frankly. If you don't think you'll be able to negotiate anal in a foreign language, go online and ask for 'completa' with a girl to get everything on the menu available.

CLINICAS (MASSAGE PARLORS)

There are plenty of regular massage parlors around Brazil but you shouldn't struggle to tell whether the one you are going into is legitimate or not. The main clue is that regular masseuses don't wear stockings or have a bowl of condoms at the ready.

These will often be called 'Massagems' but you shouldn't expect a proper sexy Thai massage. These places are little more than brothels most of the time and they are the cheap fix for horny locals. They tend to offer a strictly in-and-out service, but if you are looking to save money they might be the place to go.

These are the most like the kind of experience you get in a place like Amsterdam, only without the strict levels of hygiene and professionalism. If you are happy with the grime then at a starting price of 1 real a minute (r30 for 30 minutes) you won't be able to do much better for value.

Finding them can be difficult on their own but they are often listed in the classified sections of *O Globo* and *O Dia.*

If instead of having sex with a girl you just wanted to watch someone else have sex with her or have her dance for you in front of a booth then one of the peep shows or live sex shows might be more your sort of thing.

Live sex shows like the sort you see in Amsterdam or in Thailand involving ping pong balls and bananas in vaginas (or allegedly donkeys in Mexico) are not quite as common in Brazil, but if there's demand they will happen.

Many strip clubs are accommodating to putting on a show where you can watch a women have sex with a man or woman on stage. For some places it is a regular feature, and in others you might be able to ask for it for a price. It's by no means a very common type of entertainment.

Peep shows are a little more common in the bigger cities. They are usually built like mini entertainment complexes where you can watch pornographic movies in a masturbation booth if that holds some attraction for you in the age of the internet.

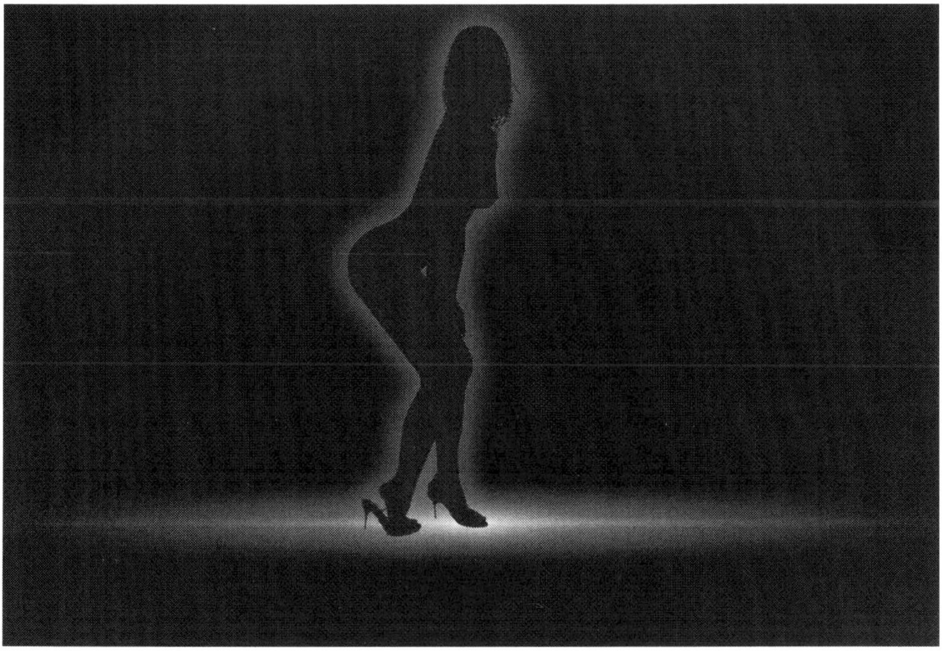

If you want to see a girl you will often have two options. The first is taking a seat in a booth around a rotating stage with other guys jacking it to the left and right of you. Or, alternatively, you can choose a private show where you pick a girl and she will dance and perform in a booth of your choosing. Multiple girls are available to perform at once for you.

You may sometimes be allowed to touch, suck, or penetrate the girls, or perhaps not. These places make more sense when you factor in that they are very cheap and they are built with locals in mind.

To you it might seem odd to pay r20 to masturbate to some girls in a booth when you could pay r200 to have sex with one, but if those prices were in dollars, pounds, or Euros it would be a more difficult choice.

Some of the larger sex shops might also offer viewing booths and peep shows, but even in Brazil these kinds of things are on the decline in recent times.

LOVE MOTELS

Love motels or hotels are something a little different in Brazil than you might be familiar with. They are not quite the themed naughty weekend retreats they are in America and they aren't quite as wholesome as the love hotels you might find in Japan.

True, some say that these places exist because many people live in very crowded homes around Brazil and a place where they can come to have sex in private is useful -- which is the story they stick to in cities like Tokyo.

Yet with some of them you will get a distinct feeling that in Brazil they are here for banging prostitutes and not much else. They might not be the most romantic getaways.

Many regular hotels will not let you bring girls back to your room and it's usually not an idle threat. This might seem a bit unfair, but keep in mind that hotels where it was allowed could very well have a line of girls waiting out the front most nights.

In-call rooms for girls a less common in Brazil, so your options are to either have a self-catering apartment that you can what you like with, to get a hotel that will let you have guests, or to pick a love motel that you can rent out by the hour.

Motels vary in how long they let you take a room. Some will charge you by the hour and others will let you rent out a room for several hours or even a whole night if you wish.

The types of rooms available come in all shapes and sizes. You can get a cheap and not so cheerful room for just a few reals an hour where you'll get little more than a clean bed. However, you can also get rooms with Jacuzzis, saunas, and even special sexual apparatus like a sex swing.

If you want to spend a bit more time with a girl you might want to hang out by a pool or chill out in a sauna. Some of the motels are quite luxurious and you won't feel uncomfortable spending time in them or hanging out with your new girlfriend for a few hours.

It is important when you pick up a girl that you have a motel ready in your mind. Letting her or a taxi driver pick might not always end in the best results for your wallet.

THE LANGUAGE BARRIER

Within this guide we'll do our best to recommend classier places where the host and some of the girls will speak a smattering of English, but beach resorts and working girls don't just make their money on gringos.

Brazil is a big enough country that many are happy enough to get by with only Portuguese and there are no assurances that most people will speak a little English.

Even when girls do speak English things can be difficult to communicate. If you chose to just stick to termas it might not be a problem as money always talks and you'll be able to sign your way into the sex pad.

At clubs or on the street things can be trickier. If you're not a confident negotiator in English then with a street savvy working girl you'll probably get eaten alive. This isn't a bad thing, prices are still good and you'll just end up paying gringo plus fees. However there are things you can do to help you get ahead of the game.

We'll start with a phrase book and then look to using it to seduce and interact with the girls.

Getting the hang of some basic Portuguese is going to be essential to talking to girls in Brazil and if you have some experience with Spanish or Italian pronunciation of it shouldn't be too out of reach.

As an English speaking gringo you really have two choices. You can take a language course before you go, or you can memorize the pronunciation of a few words. Speak slowly and use your fingers and body language a lot.

The letter 'O' on its own should be pronounced as an 'ooh', words beginning with 'qu' should be pronounced as a 'kwa' sound,

Here are some of your basic phrases

Hello – Ola

Bye – Adeus

Please – Por Favor

Thanks – Obrigado

Yes – Sim

No – Nao

English? – Fala Ingles?

How much? – Quanto custa?

How? – Como?

Who? – Quem?

What? – O Que?

Beach – Praia

Nightclub – Boate

Hotel – hotel

Drink -- Beber

Boring – Chato

Fun – Divertido

Liar – Mentisoro

I like you/like this – gostoso

What is your name? – Como se chama/Qual e o seu nome?

Beautiful -- bonito

Numbers

One – Uma

Two – Dois

Three – Tres

Four – Quatro

Five – Cinco

Six – Seis

Seven – Sete

Eight – Oito

Nine – Nove

Ten – Dez

Extracurricular vocabulary

Do you – Voce faz

Everything -- Tudo

Condom – Camisinha

Anal sex – sexo anal/culo

Player/ladies man/naughty – Safado

Two girls – Quero duplas

Ass – Bumbum/Rabo

Breasts – Tetas/Laranjas

Vagina – Buceta

Penis – Pica

Sex – Comer (to fuck)/Foder/Meter

Orgasm – Orgasmo

Enjoy (sexual) – Gozar

Cum/Ejaculate – Gozo/Porra/Ejacular

Blowjob – Boquete/Chupar

Saucy girl – Chica

Slut – Puta

Fuck me – Me come

I'll go down on you – Vou te chupar

Cariocas – black person or dark skinned

Even if you have these words down it can be difficult to really use them properly in conversation. Master a few and then get ready to let her lead the way. In more population clubs and destinations there will be plenty of girls that can speak some English.

If not it is still quite common for gringos to come to Brazil seeking ladies of the night and they know you have quite a bit of money compared to the locals. They'll make the effort.

In general when it comes to speaking to girls in Brazil it might not be as easy as it seems upfront. Foreign men don't always have the best reputation in Brazil and as you are reading a sex guide to this country you might be able to guess why.

The less English a girl speaks the less receptive she is likely to be towards foreign men (meaning she might actually speak more English than she lets on). When it comes to working girls they will usually display that Brazilian fieriness you've come here for.

Culturally Brazilians tend to like firmness and being direct. They are not as into pussyfooting around issues and if they like you they will let you know and if they don't that might also be clear. You will not be expected to enter quite the same courtship ritual of impressing a girl, but equally she will expect you to not be too reserved with your feelings. This also means you don't need to play weird text messaging games or go on four non-dates first.

Grand gestures and being too flashy might not go down as well as you'd expect in a country that brought the world carnival. Brazilians have a way of being direct that is perfectly relaxed. It's not done to be aggressive or short with someone, but because it's less confusing and more simple.

Making more of an effort with your appearance is something that will be appreciated in Brazil. You might not need to put too much on at the beach but if you want girls fighting over you at the club trying a little harder than an oversized t-shirt and sandals will be necessary.

HOOKER ETIQUETTE AND STAYING SAFE

The Brazil sex scene is not one that really wants you to be passive as it is in other places. There is certainly room to be shy and reserved, but the point and fuck method might not hit as well here as it will in other countries (though no doubt it will work).

Not only will girls expect you to interact with them but they'll also work on dragging you on up to their level of passion. Nevertheless, you are a paying customer here and you should feel comfortable to act however you want.

You will want to learn a few customs with the girls in Brazil though to ensure you have a good time, to spot girls that might cause you a problem, and in general just to stay safe.

Common sense should prevail here and if things don't seem right or you feel you are about to step into a situation that is far beyond your control – listen to the common sense. There are always more girls to find.

You needn't be paranoid about safety and scams, but there are definitely people that are more than happy to rip you off and less obvious situations that are best to avoid.

THINGS TO WATCH OUT FOR

When you are out, especially in a more risqué part of town, you will want a passport or a very good copy of your passport (or at least some form of ID). It's not uncommon for police to stop and check your ID and if you don't have one it turns out one of the best ways of getting around that is a small bribe.

Drugs can get you into a few issues in Brazil so if you are going to take any avoid carrying them around in public and be discreet. It's not hard to get them but it's also not hard for a cop to shake you down and demand a bribe. Even marijuana is tightly controlled here and as a wild Westerner you might be a target.

Besides those concerns the general scams that happen to tourists should be watched out for. People in the street are rarely trying to help you and back alleys should always be avoided at night. Keep to yourself, be ready to walk away from a person you don't know and stay in well lit areas and you should be completely fine.

SCAMS

When it comes to the girls there are a few scams to watch out for that nearly all involve going with a girl to a love motel. If you avoid taking a girl back to your hotel that can help solve a few concerns – you're very unlikely to get robbed by a girl, but she might pocket some cash she saw lying around.

When you do take a girl back to a motel only keep a little more cash than you are happy to spend (which helps with haggling) and always remember to pay after you've had your fun. You shouldn't ever give money to a girl at a club or on the way to the motel. If you do so and assuming she gets to the motel with you, it may turn out that once you've had sex it is over unless you fork over a little more – no matter what you agreed.

You can show the money or leave it on a motel table, but avoid letting her pocket it.

When taking taxis around or to the club insist to go to your destination, agree a price before you set off, or ask to use the meter. Drivers get all kinds of kickbacks from clubs and girls and it may even be best to ask to just go near your destination and walk the rest of the way.

Drivers may even lie to you about your destination – telling you a club or hotel is closed or shut down. It's usually best you don't listen – especially if you've booked in advance.

The biggest scam to watch out for when it comes to the girls is one taking you for a newbie and taking advantage of that. Part of the fun with working girls is trying out new experiences and the luck of the draw, this means you'll have to get on the learning curve and have a few odd experiences before you know what you want.

In some rare cases girls will see how far they can push that. If they know you don't speak Portuguese and you're not really sure what's what yet you are susceptible to their ruses. The most common (but by no means common) ruse is for a girl to get the police involved. She may just start yelling and claiming you've mistreated her or even claim that she is underage.

She might be willing to avoid calling the police altogether if you pay her, or when they do turn up they will also be awfully chummy with the girl. Luckily a small bribe will set things straight. If you get in that situation sneaking away or refusing to engage is usually your best option.

You needn't be terrified of this happening to you so long as you are in control of the situation and you carefully screen a girl before picking one. The same is true if you were choosing a girl back home –if things seem suspicious or she's too good to be true then listen to your gut.

SCREENING - RED FLAGS

A lot of girls will try it on with a new guy so to speak. They might give you an outrageous price or ask you to pay in dollars. They might be keen to rush you out of the place, or be vague about the services you get or how long you get to spend with her.

This is a buyer's market so don't be afraid to move on. Sometimes there is a thin line between negotiation and taking advantage. Trying to rip you off a little isn't an issue (you're probably much richer than her), but her insisting that it's normal to pay in dollars or that, for example, no girls offer anal should be a red flag.

After that you should be concerned about girls that are too pushy or in too much of a hurry. If they keep asking you for extras, lots of drinks, tips for the barman, for you to use a specific taxi, to buy her gifts, or to go to her specific motel then avoid her.

Brazilian girls may be more firm and forward but they should not be aggressive, cold, or bullish with you. If she isn't making you feel comfortable then move on – this is an experience you both need to enjoy and, as cold as it might sound, this is her job.

As with anything avoid situations that are clearly too good to be true. If you've consulted a guide like this you should have a pretty sound idea of what then expect and how much to pay. If a gorgeous girl is offering you a bargain for seemingly no reason then proceed with caution. Again, this is her job; she should be making money with it.

Aside from how she is behaving towards you pay attention to other aspects of her demeanor. Does she seem on the level or slightly doped up? Working girls in Brazil can often have issues with drugs and this is avoided for several reasons. You can't be sure what to expect with someone that is high or desperate for money.

If someone doesn't seem hygienic, if they seem very uncomfortable or upset, or you get any other sign that things are off avoid her. This should really go without saying, but if you are new and lost in a trance of beer and lust you might overlook the obvious.

SCREENING – BEST PRACTICE

When choosing a girl there are some best practices to try and follow or keep in mind so you have the best time. Firstly, try not to go to these places on your own if possible (especially the clubs). Being with a friend is the best possible insurance you can have. Besides that don't carry too much cash or leave valuable handing around your room if that is where you plan to take a girl.

When it comes to the girls, try to take your time before approaching a girl and make sure you are happy with her. Try to look past any flattering light and don't get too focused on her chest.

When you've got her attention spend a little time with her. Buy her a few drinks, have a conversation as best you can, flirt, dance, and even consider feeling her up a little if the mood is right. Besides having fun and ensuring you'll actually like a girl, the idea is to make sure she's not just here to play you for money. The haggling stage shouldn't be fun on its own and she shouldn't be squeezing you for pennies.

If she starts being too pushy or starts demanding too many drinks or the like during this initial screening period move on. When you're haggling be respectful but also stick to your guns. You're here to pay someone for a good time and that's what you should be getting. These are not fragile college girls.

Make it clear what you want and have it agreed. When it's time to leave take control of what you are doing and if at any point she tries to re-negotiate you might be best ditching her.

COMMON COURTESY

If you want to have a good time it's not just about looking out for what's good for you – look out for the girls as well. If you plan to go to the same bars or clubs then rumors of your wickedness will spread between the girls.

Condoms are a good idea everywhere you meet up with girls in Brazil and for anything sexual you do. Terma girls are usually screened for STDs but besides them you're likely out of luck. Many of these girls are poor and not very well educated – you can almost certainly convince a few to go bare, but you do so knowing the risks are quite high.

Remember not to be hypocritical when it comes to drugs. If you're too drunk or high to conduct yourself safely then wait until you've sobered up a little before hitting up a girl.

When it comes to haggling and negotiation don't try to overstep your mark and push for an insultingly low price. You should have an understanding of what your money is worth and what is a normal price (she will know both). If you are pushing really hard to pay as much for an hour with a beautiful woman as the price of a Big Mac then you might be going too far.

Girls remember who you are and talk about how much you've paid for a girl. If you come back the next night and try to pay much less for a girl she will know you're either insulting her or being cheap if you got a fair deal the night before.

Finally keep in mind that you get out what you put in with a girl. If you're limp and passionless don't expect a mind-blowing experience with a girl. She can only bring so much to the table. Learn the difference between being firm and disrespectful and between being gentle and timid.

Don't renegade or your negotiations either. If you didn't agree to anal sex then don't insist on it if she wants payment after you've made it to the hotel room.

FORTALEZA

The first stop on the tour of Brazil's love scene is Fortaleza which sits on the northeast coast. It is a well known tourist resort around the world and holds this position by having perfect weather year round and relatively low prices – even for Brazil.

It is not a place known for its important historical landmarks, but more for its buzzing beaches and fantastic restaurants and facilities for tourists. Some of the beaches can be a little less than appetizing to swim in and you get bothered by the usual touts and tat slingers, but Praia do Futuro and parts of Beira Mar are nice stretches to have a bathe.

What this does mean is that there are some really fantastic party beaches with cheap beer and dancing well into the night, and working girls available as easily as a beachside snack.

Being a seaside town you can get some really fresh and delicious seafood especially around Varjota. It has some very attractive old buildings along the seafront to stroll around (which you can see as part of the free walking tour) as well as a cathedral, a handful of museums, and some pleasant green areas if you want a break from the sand and sun.

Fortaleza is not a town that hides its main attractions very hard though and that is the girls that line up around every bar or club whether it is one made for sex or not. Tourists from all over the world come here with one thing in mind and they don't have to look far to get it.

If you're a single man on the beachfront here it is assumed quite simply what your interests are. If you want picking nothing but beach and street girls will keep you quite content and there is a good selection here.

This has an unfortunate effect of meaning regular Brazilian girls will avoid you and stay out of some of the main clubs, but if that's what you're after then Fortaleza maybe shouldn't be your first destination. You may get disappointed that some of the beach dwellers are actually other Brazilian tourists and not up for playing with you.

GETTING IN AND AROUND FORTALEZA

The easiest way to get to Fortaleza from most other major cities is by flying (with the exception of Natal which is only an 8 hour bus ride).

The airport is well served and has regular flights to most destinations. If you are coming in from abroad your best options for direct flights are Miami, Lisbon, Rome, or Amsterdam. Being at the top of the country Fortaleza can be a good place to start your Brazilian adventure or to relax for a while if you want some cheap fun. However, it's by no means Brazil's premiere destination.

From the airport there is a bus that will take you directly into the main station in 30 minutes or so, or you can choose to take a taxi for between r25 or r40. Once you are there you really only have the option of buses or taxis to get around (including the bike/rickshaw taxis known as 'motto taxis').

For most tourists sticking to the beachfront is all they are interested in and it's probably the safest and easiest option going. Some of the outer slums in Fortaleza are not the homeliest places for gringos.

Once you've got a hotel picked out you can usually walk to and from most beaches if you want to make a day of it. Buses serve the area well and you can go almost anywhere for r2 one way. The circular line operates 24 hours a day and you can check online for their status.

Regular taxis are quite good in Fortaleza and they should be running on a meter with separate daytime and night time meters. Prices start at around r4 and should be about r2 for every kilometre on top of that. If you want to stay safe keep to the well populated beaches at night and use taxis once it gets dark.

THE SCENE

Fortaleza has a good mix of sex clubs, street girls, and termas for you to try. Being cheaper it does not attract the best talent in the country and it knows the trade it plies is for tourists that won't be coming back. However there are lots of ways to have a good time here for excellent value.

Fortaleza is very popular with Italians and other southern Europeans as well as the local Brazilians. Don't expect English to be spoken too freely but there is still more than enough fun to be had.

Most of the hotels along the beachfront are not girl friendly (and they are strict about enforcing this rule) and you'll have to put up with a few of love motels not so far away. Some of the hotels you may want to scout in advance include Hipnose Motel, Ele & Ela Motel, and Dream's Motel. Getting an apartment might be the best way to go.

Most of the action happens along Beira Mar and especially around Praia de Iracema. The McDonald's was famous for a long time as the go to place to find girls, wait until later at night to find the real talent coming out.

STREET GIRLS

You should be able to spot the working girls fairly easily and they can be seen where most tourists start to congregate. If you're on the hunt Avenida Abolicao, Praia de Meireles, and near the cathedral at Praia do Passeio Publica are good.

Looking outside both the sex clubs and regular clubs after 10pm will allow you to pick from a large pool of girls most nights of the week. Expect to pay at least r100 for a nice girl and frequently as much as r200 (if you're not great at haggling) as the scene has begun to dry up.

There are lots of reports of the police hassling people in these areas, so keep everything kosher and conduct yourself well.

CLUBS

There is a mix of clubs available to try out to find girls to spend the night with. Not all of them are of fantastic quality and none stand at as the perfect destinations to attend but they are worth checking out to get your bearings.

Try to keep in mind that this is primarily a party town and that is the audience they are catering for. If you want something more reserved try an escort directory or avoid Fortaleza altogether. There are lots of nice beaches in Brazil.

Forro Mambo

Forro Mambo is the biggest club that still remains open and has a mixed selection of girls on offer. The drinks are a little overpriced and the reggae music isn't to everyone's taste but your choices are relatively limited.

This place is open to late and many of the girls will come here after they've finished up around the other bars and streets.

Zipi

Zipi is a more relaxing place to hang out and to consider starting out the night. You need to buy a drink for r10 to get in and is probably the go-to place on a regular day for the best girls going. There is a range of old and young girls here and you are looking at around r150 for an hour.

Piratas

Most of the time Piratas is a legit club but on a Monday night it brings in working girls and they are all nearly available to be taken home with you. These nights are more like the big clubs in Rio and they make the most of them by having a stronger selection of girls than either Forro or Zipi.

Armazem

Like Piratas they only have girls in on specific nights – for Armazem this is Wednesday. Again the selection of freelancers is a bit better on these nights and you can have to have them be a bit naughtier on these nights than the other big clubs.

In Fortaleza the termas are not well renowned and many are more like a mix of massage parlors without the same level of luxury that you might get in Rio. Still, there are some good options worth trying out and the privees offer some good prices for a quick session.

Sometimes the privees are a bit off the beaten track so make sure you are comfortable heading out there before you get in the taxi.

Rua Sen Madureira

At this privee you'll find a few levels of girls that will offer massages and extras – including full sex and a blowjob. The reason to come here is the fact that it is only r60 for 30 minutes. The low price reflects what you get in terms of selection, but you can luck out and get something more special.

Anny Massagens

This is one of the bigger massage parlors in the area and while it doesn't get the best ratings in the world it gives you what you want. You get a less than perfect massage and sex for less than r100 – a little bit pricey for what is available.

RECIFE

Moving a little further down the north coast from the cheap thrills of Fortaleza we come to the beach city of Recife. Recife has a bit more going for it than just being a cheap hangout for horny Europeans – it's known as the Venice of Brazil thanks to its mix of pretty islands and canals.

It is a large city with a similar amount of inhabitants as Fortaleza and the greater area known as Grande Recife is very large and arguably the fifth largest in Brazil.

The city has a nice mix of excellent beaches as well as some fascinating churches and tourist attractions. Even if you come here for its sex scene it is worth visiting some of its forts or museums during the day.

Boa Viagem Beach has a reputation the world over as one of the best city beaches to visit and is enormous at nearly eight kilometers long. It also has the smaller and more relaxed Pina Beach and Teimosa Beach if Boa Viagem is wearing you down with all its hot bodies and beach vendors.

The surrounding towns of Olinda (just a short walk away) and Porto de Galinhas are fascinating places to visit and it has grown itself into becoming on the best tourist destinations in Brazil. However, thanks to this it's no longer has the scene it once did (dropping single men in favor of families) and it's included here to give you the low down on an area you might otherwise want to visit thanks to all its attractions.

Nevertheless, Recife still has plenty to offer on the sex front and you can happily mix sightseeing with pleasure.

GETTING IN AND AROUND

Unless you're staying in the surrounding area flying is generally the best way to get into Recife. Natal can be reached in 4 hours by bus (and arguably has a better scene) so it might be worth incorporating it into your trip. Recife is also a popular cruise stop if that is of any interest to you.

Recife's airport is very well appointed and preferable to some of the dingier ones in its neighboring coastal resorts. There are regular flights to cities all over Brazil as well as regular flights to Miami, Paris, Lisbon, Milan, Madrid, Frankfurt, and Amsterdam. It has the distinction of being slightly cheaper to reach from Europe than a few of the other big cities in Brazil.

Getting into the city from the airport is easy and safe with the subway and there are airport bus shuttles which can get you straight to the big beaches and the city centre in 20 to 30 minutes.

Recife isn't a large city so around the beachfront you can walk to many destinations if you plan your day in advance. Otherwise taxis are easy to find and will serve you well as long as you stick to the meter. Consider taking them after dark as ground reports suggest Recife isn't the safest city out there and make sure you don't pay them in huge bills if you want to be sure of change.

The buses are easy to use and if you are planning to scoot around the city a lot tickets can be used on the subway as well. You shouldn't need to use the subway too much outside of getting to and from the airport however.

On Sundays it can get a little dead around Recife city centre so try not to hang around on your own too much and consider visiting one of the smaller towns nearby. This is Brazil after all.

Some have had great experiences in Recife thanks to its smaller scene and preference for privates. Others have had one could be best described as ordeals. In the past it was a town that could rival Fortaleza and Natal for talent and action, but now it has only one or two clubs that are quite expensive and a smaller strip of girls around the beach front.

Much of the action is found along Boa Viagem and especially around the Sampa club and the Domingos Ferreira behind it which is usually home to between 50 and 100 girls on a given night. More so than a few of the other locations in this guide the girls are season – if you come in the off season expect slim pickings which balance out potentially lower prices.

You will also find a few girls outside Franciscan Convent of Saint Anthony looking for a lay, but for some reason, as in most of Brazil, the girls outside churches tend not to be the classiest. There are few clubs that are worth visiting nearby as well.

Like many of these beach towns the hotels are not accommodation to bringing girls back and you won't find much in the way of luxury Termas or super-dome sex nightclubs.

Reports have been growing of police in the area working with girls and pimps with the underage trick and forcing guys to pay up or prove their innocence. Going out with a friend is a very good idea and you should generally avoid speaking to girls via a pimp or helpful stranger. It's not good for her, the trade, or your wallet.

Still the selection of girls here is generally felt to be quite good if limited and sometimes more expensive thanks to the dwindling completion (though a girl for r100 is still possible if you look around).

Sampa

Sampa is the biggest and one of the most established clubs in Recife and is generally the go to place to find girls on any given night in Recife. It doesn't get busy until much later in the night and there is a cover charge of r30.

Compared to some of the other clubs which don't try too hard to get girls in Sampa is godsend. You can usually find a girl (of about 30 to 50 that hang around) here for around r150 for an hour before you take her to a love motel or your apartment. Some say they've been paying as much as r400 and in general the drinks and food are overpriced.

If you get there too early you can look around for the girls there. Recife has a bit of a culture of street girls being picked up in cars and you might get led to a slightly more expensive taxi if you pick one up here. This is a bit more of a seller's market so expect the girls to be feistier. R100 for an hour is about right and try to make sure you've agreed upfront how much you want to pay.

Ninfas

This is the other big club that is still open and running in Recife. There is a relatively large cover of r50 and drinks are, again, slightly overpriced. You will not find such a large selection as you often get at Sampas but Ninfas has a slightly more relaxed atmosphere.

Like Sampas getting here early will leave you with slim pickings in terms of girls that may be more likely to be older or out of shape. If you want an easy night it's not a bad choice, but expect to more for less here.

Esetica Graceiete

This is one of the larger and better known brothels in Recife (thought it has several you can check out that are similarly unimpressive as each other). It is located along Boa Viagem and is a standard massage parlor starting at r40 for a massage and handjob and r100 for full sex.

The girls tend not to be the most inspiring but if you push they'll have a good range of 4 to 6 girls who make pique your taste. The massages aren't of the highest quality, but you won't beat Graceiete for value as there are no real extras and no need for a room. It's clean, safe, easy and a good option if you've burned out on the street scene.

Casa Blanca

Casa Blanca is run more like a typical brothel that you'd find in Europe. You go in to a seated area with a few girls posing themselves on a sofa before choosing one and taking them to a room of your choice. You pay per room which range from r150 to r250.

The facilities are simple but well-kept and clean. There is even a bar and lounge area you can relax in if you wish. Not quite a Rio Terma but if you like the girls here you might feel like returning.

SALVADOR

Moving down the coast once again you get to Salvador – a very Brazilian beach city that is popping with colors and a vibrant party scene. It's more than just a cheap seaside resort and is becoming something of a hip hangout these days.

The people are renowned across Brazil for being laidback and it is generally much calmer and safer than some of these other resorts. It's the third largest city in Brazil and as such there is a lot going on.

It's not quite competing with Rio or Sao Paulo as a must-see city in Brazil, but many visitors that come here find it's their favorite of the big cities. The city is split into its cliff side half and the bay side half which are intersected with some true colonial architecture. The best examples are the central squares Praca da Se and Terreiro de Jesus that are shadowed by a cathedral.

There is a good collection of museums and churches to visit when getting the feel of the city and some markets and interesting restaurants to try out. Salvador is a city made for sitting back and enjoying its views more so than sunbathing, but it has some very clean and relaxing beaches including Porto de Barra beach.

Flamengo and Stella Maris are equally well equipped and good places for safe swimming compared to Fortaleza's murky waters and Recife's shark infestation.

To many the city is most famous for its live music scene with classic Brazilian Samba and modern genres making an appearance as well as allegedly the largest Carnival in the world usually around February. If you really want to party it's a great time to come, but expect higher prices for everything and streets thick with tourists.

Getting in and around

Salvador isn't great for getting buses unless you're happy to save a few dollars to spend an entire day of your life on a slow moving bus. The airport is a large one that is well served by the rest of Brazil and you can get good value flights to much of continental Europe as well as many other South American countries.

The airport is about 30 to 40 minutes outside of the city centre and you can get there by taxi, shuttle bus, or air conditioned mini bus. In Salvador the taxis are either metered or they come with preset price menus of various destinations. These latter taxis are known as 'executive' taxis and while they don't always give you the best price they do give you a fair one.

Meter taxis will often haggle rather than use the meter so they are easier, but more expensive, but they are always there for you to use.

The bus will only cost you r3 one way but finding the bus stop on the other side of the airport car park can be a challenge.

The city has its own train station and metro but as with many of the beach cities you'll likely not need to venture too far into the suburbs they mostly serve. Much of the old city is easily navigable by foot and there are buses to get you around the coast and beaches with only a little bit of a headache. Be careful that the buses don't stop running too early.

One note of caution is that Salvador is quite a fractured and spread out city. Things are not centered on one main beach in the way they are in some other Brazilian cities. If you're not careful a taxi ride can take much longer than you think it will – make sure to have a motel arranged or never stray too far from your apartment.

THE SCENE

Salvador is a large and vibrant city so the scene is quite large if not the most exciting in all of Brazil. There are always new clubs and private houses coming up and old ones shutting down.

Salvador has a bit of a reputation as an unsafe town to hang around, but in truth it's not much worse than many other Brazilian cities. You just need to keep your wits about you and follow common sense. Avoid dark alleys at night and stick to girls you trust after going out with friends you know.

Going out in town there is a wide selection of girls, a slightly more relaxed policy about taking girls back to your room, and a few clubs that aren't Rio big, but do their own things fairly well. For girlfriend motels try out Oasis Motel, Fantasy Motel, Motel Kamasutra and Motel Charm (they're not exactly known for their inventive names).

Luckily many of the main scenes of action are in fairly friendly and safe areas so you can browse and flirt at your own pace. It is said that Salvador is a place to come if you are interested in non-professionals – the locals are less hung-up on the idea of sleazy foreigners, they are characteristically friendly and open, and it's the best place in Brazil to find dream girls with caramel skin and big assets.

The main beach Porto da Barra is the main area for meeting girls in the city. Pelourinho, Pitbua, and Itapu are also great neighborhoods to try out if pickings are thinning out at the main beach as are the outside of the bigger clubs.

If you come to Salvador after hitting up Rio or even some of the biggest hotspots in the world, you may be surprised by how amateurish the girls in Salvador can be. If they are more serious about the game they will usually move on to a bigger city.

Far from being a bad thing, this means you can often haggle for lower prices and get a true girlfriend experience. Here in Salvador that doesn't just mean a hooker that will kiss you on the lips and pretend to like you – as it does in many other parts of the world. It can mean a week long companion that you keep returning to without having to go scouting again.

Expect to pay as much as r300 for a girl in one of the fancier clubs and to get as cheap as r20 for half an hour of naughty fun if you go to an in-and-out parlor in the centre of the city.

Fridays and Saturdays are usually the busiest days of the work week when it comes to girls, but you'll be assured of finding someone to meet your tastes.

If you're not going to be mongering every day it is best to arrange to come to Salvador on those two days to get the most out of them. Some of the other cities are not quite so dependent on the weekend for trade.

CLUBS AND TERMAS

With its live music scene and less of a reliance on professionals you'll often find that the Salvador scene works a lot out of regular bars and venues (known as casa de shows).

Some are well known for having girls working there such as the Bambara but things are not so in your face as they are in classic sex clubs. If a girl is alone she is usually working as a garota (independent prostitute) and you will have to go over and speak to them.

There is not likely to be a bar fine for leaving, but you will have to pick up her tab for the night. You may like to just get her number and arrange to meet at another time and just pay for the time you do spend with her.

Rio Vermehlo is the place to go for these legit clubs with girls that are willing to meet you. Head over to Pituba for a large selection of parlors and strip clubs that will help you meet your needs. Orla is notorious for its strip clubs which aren't as classy as they purport to be, but certainly are priced that way anyway.

Eros

Eros is a classic club and a well known one in the area. You need to pay an entrance fee of r50 and you are looking anywhere from r100 to r300 to take a girl home for the night. If you come a bit later in the night, especially on a Friday or Saturday, you'll find you can get girls for much less than that.

Morganas Massagem

This is something of an infamous massage parlor in the city. It's cheap and quite difficult to find for beginners as it's not well signed. It is simply labeled number 40 at the Largo Sao Pedro.

Here you will face a lineup of girls and then you are free to take one to a room to have your fun at r50 for 30 minutes without any extras. Get there early as the girls are all put out at once and it's first-come-first-served.

Café Bangkok

Bangkok is fairly central and does a good job of selecting girls and putting on other types of entertainment. On busier nights it will have as many as 20 women available and it is close to the airport so you can make this your first stop into the big city of Salvador.

RIO DE JANEIRO

So we've made it to what many think of as the sex capital of the world. There is a fantastic selection of women every night and a collection of genuinely luxurious clubs to meet women at. This is the place that dreams come true and if you want there is no reason to ever leave this city when you visit Brazil.

Rio is essentially a giant metropolis built on a tropical paradise with some of the best beaches in the world stretching out under the wondrous Sugar Loaf Mountain and the Corcovado Peak. This harbor is often included as one of the natural wonders of the world alongside Everest, the Grand Canyon, and the Great Barrier Reef. All of this with Christ the Redeemer looking over it all.

Despite its fame Rio is neither the capital of Brazil (that is Brasilia) nor the largest (that honor goes to Sao Paulo), but it still dwarfs many cities in the world with 6 million in the main city and 12 million in the wider Rio area.

The city is split into five districts with the two most important to you being the Centro district which is home to the city's business district and old city, and the Zoma Sul (south zone) which is home to the Copacabana and the Ipanema – two of the most iconic beaches on the planet.

It is likely these beaches where you spend much of your stay in Rio and it's where Cariocas (the people of Rio) spend much of their time as well. Rio is not a city that divorces beach life as something for tourists and the weekend – it is a city whose culture mixes together beach and the everyday.

The sands on many of them are kept soft and clean and you'll find everything you need to keep you fed and entertained along the golden coastline. Not all of them are great for meeting girls and drinking beer – the bay beaches like Flamengo and Botafogo are more for looking at. Aside from the two famous beaches mentioned you can also try out Vemelha, Barra da Tijuca, and the nudist beach Abrico.

Once you've had your fill of coconuts, empanadas, and sand you'll no doubt want to check out the surrounding mountains and hills, some of the city's fine cathedrals, its unique shopping districts, and some classy history and

art museums. And in-between all of that you'll have all the girls your heart could desire.

Come for Carnival and the New Year's Eve part for two of the biggest city celebrations in existence.

GETTING IN AND AROUND

Like a lot of the Brazilian cities flying is by far the best way to get into Rio. Galeao International Airport is only 30 minutes outside of the city centre and there are daily flights to all the major cities in Europe including London and Rome. It's also accessible from Atlanta, New York, Miami, Toronto, and Dallas.

Getting away from the airport your best option is a bus or shuttle service from your hotel. The Premium bus to Zona Sul (where most of the hotels are) is only r16, and if you want to live cheap the BRT Transcarioca buses will get your there for r3.

If you want to take a taxi then push past all the touts and crazies from the departure lounge and get to an empty yellow taxi that isn't gunning for you. Ask to use the meter and then expect to pay r60 to get to Zona Sul.

The Santos Dumont Airport is in the very centre of the city and it is your home to the rest of Brazil with daily flights to all of the major cities for good prices if you book in advance.

For a gringo taxis are often the easiest way to make trips that aren't to the big tourist destinations or along the main beaches. Uber is available in Rio and is a great alternative to be sure of how much you are paying if you can get the internet working on your mobile provider (wi-fi is surprisingly abundant in Rio however).

The most common taxis are the yellow variety and it's best to take them from a taxi rank and will charge you r2 for each kilometer you make on top of the r5 you pay for sitting in. Make sure you are going by the meter when you get in or risk haggling for twice the price when you get there.

Even in Brazil traveling by taxi is expensive so consider using the bus or subway where you can (not great for impressing girls though). The buses can be very confusing to manage as there are so many lines and providers each costing about r4 for a ride. Sightseeing tours for tourists are some of the easiest and most stress-free ways of seeing the city.

The subway is thankfully easier to navigate and the signage is not so confusing. If you are staying for a while you can get an electronic card which will give you one-way rides for r4. It serves many of the big stops and locations and is safer and easier than many other roots.

The subway and walking should be fine for the beaches and use taxis for the rest of your nights out.

THE SCENE

Most other cities, with the exception of Sao Paulo, are just weaker version of the Rio scene. As in the other locations you can meet girls out on the beach, at a parlor, or in a club, but here you get an enormous selection of the best of the best.

There is a lot of competition for your custom and the girls know that to stand out they have to be the best and embody that carnival magic. For a long time the club Help was famous nearly the world over for offering herds of the sexiest girls around, but now it has fallen and been replaced with some smaller competitors.

No matter the constant claims of Rio's former glory you can't beat the combination of beach and babes. You'll find girls all over but there is never any real need to leave the Copacabana area by any stretch to find what you are looking for.

And here the services you get are all night long and you are far less likely to run into scams or con-girls. Though, keep in mind, you will still need to stay on your toes.

As already stated Copacabana and the stretch of Ipanema beach near it are the best places to locate yourself for your stay (Leblom is also a decent choice). Here you'll find lots of accommodation at relatively good prices. Apartments are in abundance which will let you bring girls back (though you will often be surrounded by residents) or you have the options of using hotels and motels.

In Rio hotels are sometimes a little better at letting you bring girls back but they may also charge you a r50 fee for the privilege of doing so. That might sound like a rip-off, but if you'd prefer it to visiting a love motel then it's not a bad deal at all.

Rio is all about choice when it comes to girls and as a general rule of thumb the Termas have the best selection of girls and you don't need a room, the clubs will have a big mixture of girls (good if you have particular tastes) and the beach girls tend to be the cheapest and easiest during the day before moving to a club at night.

Large stretches of Copacabana have girls working it during both the day and night. If you want to visit a restaurant or bar where the girls will hang out look around Avenue Atlantica. The famous 'hooker beach' stretch of Copacabana is found outside the Othon Palace hotel. Head over to the sand and get yourself a seat for a few reals and wait for the girls to walk on by.

You can usually take them home for r150 after a bit of haggling and avoid the pimp translators. If your Portuguese isn't great you may want to buddy up with someone that will help you out or bite the bullet and let someone help translate. If that hassle turns you off then you can simply go to a terma or club where talking isn't quite as important.

The massagems are open from midday to later at night but usually close when the clubs get going after 10pm. Things are very cheap and quick in the massagems on the Copacabana. You won't have to haggle too much and you can get in and out in 40 minutes with full sex for r100 or under.

Vila Mimosa isn't on the Copacabana but it is arguably the most famous red light district in the city (the Copacabana transcends the idea entirely). To get there you need to go to the central area of the city near Sotero de Reis. When you get there you'll find some of the scariest and cheapest prostitutes in the city.

It is not for the faint hearted and makes men out of boys and mincemeat out of your junk. They work like an open air massagem and you can get services for under r50 with usually a room fee of about r10. You simply visit one of the bars in the area and then pick a girl of your liking for little more than pocket change.

Despite the sleazy reputation there is security around so it is relatively safe and you'll most likely only find trouble if you cause it. The district has been under constant threat of closure for years so make sure it hasn't been turned into a shopping mall before you turn up there.

Finally, there are the termas which are really only done right here in Rio. By far the best option for a relaxed environment, pretty girls, and the ability to see samba performed as it was meant to be. Several of the biggest and best are available via the beachfront and the prices aren't bad either.

The only reason you wouldn't want a terma is if you are into some kinkier stuff, you are really into discretion (good luck in Rio), or you are looking for a girlfriend for the night.

The prices mentioned here were about average during Olympic fever so you are more likely to get a bargain now that things have calmed down.

Mosaic

In the wake of Help's closure several places are looking to take up its mantle and Mosaic is one of biggest contenders. It is a classic club scene with girls dancing like crazy inside and waiting to flirt with you before you take them home.

You pay a different cover fee depending on the night, usually about r30, and you can use that cover fee as credits for drinks (so you can get r30 worth of drinks). If you come nearer the weekend you'll find as many as 50 girls here – it's no Help, but it's still a big selection. Mosaic is a little harder to get to because it's near Vila Mimosa, but it's still a good option if you want to try that area.

Barberella

Barberlla isn't the best club to have graced Rio but it is a solid place with an r80 entrance free which gives you two drinks when you get in. There is usually a good selection of cuties in there and a more vibrant dance scene. Barberella likes to get in DJs that know how to set things off.

Expect a bar fine of r80 if you want to take one of the girls out with you. Some people have complained about unfair bar tabs so make sure to keep an eye on what you are actually ordering here.

Mabs

Mabs is a bar and club on the Copacabana strip that is now a popular haunt for finding barely clad girls and reasonably priced drinks. With the scene having gotten a bit smaller prices have gone up and the girls here will try it on for as much as r600 for a night. Sadly if you don't pay then another gringo might – r300 is more like it.

Nevertheless Mabs isn't a bad place to start the night to see if anything takes your fancy and it is relaxed enough that leaving without a girl isn't a big deal. It does not always have the greatest selection of girls, but the crowd changes a lot so it's quite possible you'll find a girl of your choosing if you go.

4X4 (4 por 4)

This is really the big Terma left standing in Rio and people are talking about it for good reason. It opens from 2 pm until late and may have over 100 girls at any one time showing themselves off on the dance floor or around the premises.

It is located in Centro and built to cater to the businessmen crowd which usually signifies a slightly better attitude.

There is a whisky bar with a fireman's pole that you might be lucky enough to see the girls use and a lounge and bar upstairs that you can relax in and even get some food if you enjoy.

Things can get hectic at 4X4 and it may not be the perfectly relaxed experience you want, but if you are looking for the best selection of girls in Rio and a stress-free bang then you're looking for 4X4. Expect a heavy cover charge to get in depending on the night – the going rate for most termas is about r100 to get in.

Once you get in you'll pay anywhere from r200 to r300 for a one hour session and most of the girls are tech savvy so you can get their numbers and meet them again outside the club for an all-night session if you wish.

Monte Carlo

Monte Carlo is one of the legendary termas in Rio and has been around for a long time, but luckily it offers a great service rather than it crumbling down around you.

When you arrive you'll see how it offers a different experience to 4X4 with often only 20 to 30 girls a night and not often a huge concentration of guys fighting over them. This lets you have a more relaxed and intimate approach with the girls and Monte Carlo has stayed in the game by picking some of the most exquisite girls on the Rio scene.

Terma Cancun

Cancun is a new kid on the block so it's good to go here if you want to try out the facilities before they get worn in. Like 4X4 they have a whisky bar and a fairly large collection of girls with around 50 on busy nights and a more reserved 25 on quieter evenings.

Things get better later in the night and it really does try to differentiate itself from the many other termas on the block with its services and facilities. It is new though, so expect the selection of girls to be patchy (the popular clubs usually get the best girls).

Terma MC

MC is another relatively newer terma and it takes more after the Monte Carlo model. You get the robe and rub experience and there are usually twice as many girls as there are guys at any given time.

It's really trying to make a name for itself by having excellent girls that set the online reviewers going wild. It's a good place to try your luck for a few hours you won't forget.

It costs r110 to get in and as much as r400 for a girl for one hour with the room included in that price.

Solarium

Solarium has been around for close to 40 years so it knows what it's doing. It's located in the Lapa area where many of the most buzzing clubs still set up shop.

It's smaller and a little cheaper than some of the other termas and it shows with a more personal touch. For a long time it has had a reputation as being more for locals and the club thanks their success to the repeat local business.

What does this mean? Expect girls with big behinds and to get a real Brazilian experience if you come here. Solarium is still going strong and a good contender for a terma to visit.

SAO PAULO

When we move on to this final stop things start to get cooler: literally as Sao Paulo has relatively colder weather than its northern counterparts (going down to a horrifyingly chilly 19 Celsius in June).

It is an enormous city, the largest in Brazil with 11 million living in the main city area and 20 million in its wider urban area – making it the third largest city in the world by some measures.

Thanks to the history of Brazil you'll find that in Sao Paulo people often have a much more European look about them and it is also home of Brazilian business. It is has one of the highest GDPs of any city in the world and is technically the richest city in the southern hemisphere.

Things are different here in Sao Paulo and you can feel that as you move around the city. While there are some fantastic beaches not too far away from its outskirts, it is the only city in this guide that is not a beach town. Thanks to this it has often been one of the overlooked Brazilian tourist cities.

However, calling Sao Paulo overlooked is starting to become a cliché as the rest of the world is discovering a city that more than proves it knows how to entertain and party hard without the beach life.

Thanks to its huge range of museums, restaurants, attractions, and clubs it keeps its residents and visitors more than happy. There isn't just city on offer here either as Sao Paulo is in spitting distance of the Parque Estadual Serra do Marr which puts you in touch with rainforest and mountains.

Sao Paulo (or Sampa as it is known by many) is a city of contrast and huge diversity. It is a relatively young city but unlike similarly aged cities you might find in the USA it is full of old-looking colonial buildings and architecture. All of which is surrounded by palm trees and modern skyscrapers. The people who live here are just as mixed being one of the most diverse cities in the world and home to the largest population of Japanese people outside Japan.

To make the most of Sampa you'll want to visit its old city, its new city, its many museums and theatres, and sample a few of its enormous parks. Finding your way in the city can be difficult at first but when you get orientated you'll find there is a lot to see.

Sao Paulo actually has three airports but the main airport for international flights is Guarulhos International Airport which is well served by most of the major cities in the world. You might not find the same regularity between Europe and Sampa as you do Rio and Europe but finding flights shouldn't be difficult.

Being quite southern Sao Paulo is more expensive to fly to for most people but getting between Rio and Sampa shouldn't cost more than a few hundred reals. Viracopos has some cheaper flights to Europe but it is nearly 100 kilometers away from the city so it's best to avoid it.

From Guarhulos you can get a shuttle bus to the centre for r40 and a local public bus for r10 or less. Paulista Avenue and the Jardins areas are good places to look for if you want to eat some good food and see some interesting places and buses will get you there easily. It will take you about 30 minutes to get there from the airport.

The taxis from the airport in Sampa are some of the easiest to deal with in Brazil. You'll pay as much as r120 but the prices are usually fixed and you aren't hounded in the same way you might be in Rio.

If you are going to or coming from Rio, Congonhas Airport is where you'll most likely be going and it's very easy to get to being in the centre of the city. You can easily take the metro from there.

Sao Paulo, unfortunately, is one of the hardest cities to get around in Brazil because it doesn't rest on a beach in the same way. You can't simply rest on the coast and take buses out to the bigger destinations a few times.

Luckily though the metro here is relatively easy to use and does serve most of the city well. It is clean and safe and you can pick up a wireless card to use on it for r3.50 that can be topped up and used on buses as well. Keep away from peak hours however.

The metro in Sampa is notorious for being ruthless and treating people like cattle. The bus will also get crowded in peak hour so try to move around early in the morning or after most people have gone to work. It's less than r4 to travel on the bus so planning ahead can save you money.

The white taxis in Sampa are safe and easy to find but you may find that you end up paying more for a ride than is fair. Try Uber if you want to save some money and your phone is in good order here.

While there is a huge issue with inequality in Sao Paulo it is actually one of the safer cities in Brazil thanks to its large and wealthy middle class.

THE SCENE

They say Rio is where you go to party and Sao Paulo is where you go to do business. This applies equally to their sex scene with many claiming that Rio girls are wild and will do things with their hips and to your face that you won't forget.

Sao Paulo on the other hand is more reserved – you can get anything you want with its huge choice and variety but you'll have to pay for it. In many respects the scene here is more like it is the west.

The girls are often a bit more 'professional' (not necessarily a good thing) and are looking more to get the job done. There are many millionaires in the city so some have high price tags.

Accordingly escorts are much bigger in Sampa than some of the other cities and many rely on that as a way to get the most desirable girls. Nevertheless, Rua Augusta is an enormous red light district full of clubs, termas, and freelancers.

Outside that you can also find plenty of cheap and not so cheerful parlors and private houses for a quickie and more. These can be a bit harder to find than in Rio because things are not as well grouped together. Girls have a reputation for being cheap and only doing exactly what you've agreed to in negotiations.

The biggest problem with the Sampa scene is that it's not as ready-made for tourists. Looking for clubs full of girls that speak English? You might be out of luck in some parts and more negotiation is usually expected here.

On the plus side this means the girls are catering more to the Brazilian audience and not gullible tourists. There is a huge variety of girls and you'll find you won't get messed around as much if you can get past the language barrier.

Even with the language barrier tourists mean money and gringo prices. You won't struggle to get laid in one of the clubs or termas.

The hotels here are as strict as the rest of the country for the most part (though the hotels around Paulista and the red light district are surprisingly lenient) and you'll no doubt have to hit up one of the love motels. You can try Acaso Motel, Motel Farao's, Adventure Motel, or Motel Caribe for any nightly outings.

Scandallo

Scandallo pitches itself as an upper-class joint and it comes with an entry fee of r220 to match. For that price you get entry into a well decked out building with a restaurant, bar, and dance space for girls and you also get to use a good chunk of it on food and drinks if you wish.

You don't get any of it back so spend it while you still have the chance. You will find a large selection of girls here but not necessarily the best. In some ways Scandadllo is a classic example of the Sampa scene – you pay a lot and you get treated well in a well-presented venue but the girls are lacking.

Expect to pay between r200 and r300 for a girl after you've gotten a room. To its credit Scandallo runs things tightly and you can expect large crowds if you get there later in the day.

Love Story

Love Story isn't a classic love story but rather a sweaty dance-floor filled with one of the largest collection of independent working girls in Sao Paulo. Not all the girls in here are professional or even working but there sometimes over 200 girls to pick from.

It is often said the best girls work as independents rather than as part of an agency so if you're into the party scene and you want to have a huge selection of girls then Love Story is a fantastic way to go. It's truly an all night affair with things not really heating up until the very early hours of the morning.

You can get a girl for an all night stay for r300 but you will need to buy quite a few drinks at the bar just to get in. Expect a messy night here.

Enjoy

Enjoy mixes elements of a club and a terma and is generally preferred by those in the know to the big two venues Scandallo and Miruna. It is a great place to relax and watch girls and then when you're ready you can pick up a girl for an hour for r220.

The reason it is much loved is not because it has a bigger dance floor, a better bar, or a bubblier jazuzzi, but simply because it is a contender for 'best girls in Sao Paulo'. Enjoy is definitely worth checking out.

Miruna

Miruna has been around for a while and works more like a traditional brothel than a terma. You pick your girl out of a line up and take her back to the available room. You'll need to hang around with the other guys here while you wait – so if you're looking for complete privacy you might be a little disappointed.

On most days you can expect anywhere from 10 to 20 girls with a good mix available and usually someone to meet most tastes. They go through staff quickly here though, so don't always expect a pro but Miruna is nearly always a safe bet.

In its favor it only costs r230 for a quick session with a girl and that includes most things but expect to tip an extra r50 if you want uncovered oral sex or anal – they also charge for using credit cards here.

The rooms and facilities are probably Miruna's biggest draw. They are always clean, well-presented, and comfortable to be in. If you're looking for a solid hitter with minimal fuss then Miruna is a good choice.

Tangara

Tangara is a much loved terma on the scene and the reason why is hard to put your finger on. It doesn't do any one thing particularly well but people seem to always come out having had a good time.

The girls here change very frequently but with as many as 40 girls to choose from and many of them first timers you can be sure of finding something exciting and new.

Prices in Tangara are pretty good – you can get an hour with a girl for less than r200 and the rooms are clean if nothing special. Tangara manages to put out a truly relaxing atmosphere and is well worth checking out.

Brooklin

Brooklin is a classic Terma with a well stocked whiskey bar and a great selection of girls. There's even wi-fi available here if you want to check your email: this also means phones are allowed inside.

The Morumbi area it is located in has several other large private houses with girls waiting inside but Brooklin is the main attraction. There are 30 to 40 girls there most days and a tip-top collection to be found. You'll be well treated and you will no doubt want to try out a few of them.

Expect to pay about r200 for an hour with a girl – which is fantastic value as far as Sampa goes.

Maytuna

Maytuna is what is often called a 'clinica' in Sampa and other parts of Brazil and is essentially just a massage parlor with everything that entails. Maytuna is located near the big international airport so it's good if you are in a hurry.

Maytuna is a very small place with only a few girls on offer but they make sure they nevertheless have a good selection and you can choose for a massage table quickie or something more intense in the bedroom.

One of the few places in Sama where cheap and cheerful go together.

CONCLUSION

Brazil has a lot to offer a man with the right thing on his mind and whatever is on his mind is usually on offer. It is one of the few sex destinations in the world that lives up to its reputation because the girls here are on another level. They know how to please a man and they see their job as giving you pleasure and making your dreams come true.

There may be hassle and scams, and you may get fleeced as a gringo out on the hunt for the first time, but this is part of the fun and part of the Brazil scene. It will all become worth it when you have a little chica with those hips and that silky skin spending the night with you.

To get the most out of your time here you will want to prepare in advance for it. Don't simply turn up with 1000 reals to spend on girls and then blow it in one night. Prepare in your mind what you want from the night and a girl.

You have a chance to make all of your sex dreams come true so don't waste it. Always wanted to have a go with two girls? Are you curious what it's like to be with a skinny woman? How about a larger woman? Maybe you want to be a completely different person and completely dominate a person.

Taking control of your fantasies

More so than most other sex scenes in the world, in Brazil you are really asked to take control. The girls here will feed off your energy and desires so don't let that go to waste. Come to the clubs and termas with an open mind and without shame.

People here are not out to judge you and what you're doing is seen in a different context because paying for sex is not shameful and the worlds of working girls and girlfriends are seen as worlds apart.

Getting used to this idea can take some time and to do well in Brazil you may need to shed some other ideas you've carried over with you. Being timid is not an option and being upfront about your feelings is the only way you'll get them met.

In much of the west there is a culture of almost deference to women and an idea that sexuality should be hidden away in the bedroom. When you are interested in a woman you slowly court each other without making it too obvious that you are interested (which is for some reason seen as disrespectful) and then you are not supposed to talk too much about sex when you start having it.

This is not to say that women in Brazil don't demand you to respect them, but it is to say that if you don't show any interest they will assume you are not interested and they will happily walk all over you.

If you feel you are going to struggle with this then take your time at a club, go over in your mind what you want to happen and even consider writing down all the things you would do, and be honest with a girl that you're feeling nervous.

When you come back down from the heights of Brazil you may find that these experiences have made you more confident and you are actually better able to communicate with future lovers about the things you want.

Getting the most out of your trip

It can be a mistake to base a trip to Brazil all on having sex with exotic girls at clubs. It might be your driving reason for coming here and it may be the most fun you have, but if you build your expectations up too much you will be disappointed.

Brazil may give you a taste of a life you didn't think was possible before you arrived, but Brazilian women are still only human. Pin all your hopes on finding a flawless beauty that will do anything you ask just like a beloved porn star for about $30 US and you will have those hopes dashed.

Try to treat every experience and every girl as a separate experience that should be enjoyed for what it is. Try not to constantly compare each girl you come across with the best you ever had.

There is a lot of talent all around the country and a lot to see. Clubs often don't warm up until much later at night and they can be almost dead on a Sunday in Brazil. You can spend all of your holiday hunting bars, clubs, and parlors for girls and not do any better than if you'd spent a few hours here and there.

It is a good idea to try out both the club and terma experience while you are in Brazil – especially in a city like Rio. They can be quite different with one giving you the chance to pick from an enormous room of girls and seduce them, and the other allowing you to become completely relaxed while you are treated like a sexual king.

Most of all don't forget to look beyond the sex clubs and try to meet a wider range of Brazilians. See the sights and explore the hills, rainforests, and beaches of Brazil's great cities. Eat strange and beautiful meals that use coconuts in just about every way imaginable.

Avoid becoming too intoxicated with Brazil while you are there because it's a way of living that can only sustain you for a little bit before you need to return to the real world. Keep Brazil in your mind for what it is - somewhere that can make your dreams come true, yet avoid making a fantasy of it.

Good luck and have fun on your adventures!

72025608R00055

Made in the USA
San Bernardino, CA
22 March 2018